3
Short
Plays

J. M. KESSLER

HONEY STAR PUBLISHING

ISBN: 10:0986220027
ISBN-13: 978-0986220029

DEDICATION

For Paul Casey.
And to John Lant and Will Manus, with many, many
thanks.

CONTENTS

ACKNOWLEDGMENTS

Have A Nice Day**

First production at the Jewel Box Theatre Center, Los
Angeles, CA 1999

The Tin Heart**

First production at the Jewel Box Theatre Center, Los
Angeles, CA 2000

A Rose By Any Other Name

First production at Write Act Repertory Theatre* for
New Frequency: A Theater of the Mind Radio
Theater, *Conversations In Cars* series, Los Angeles, CA
2004

**Have A Nice Day and The Tin Heart were each the result
of the Playwrights Workshop, headed by Paul Casey in
conjunction with the Los Angeles Playwrights Group and
the Jewel Box Theatre Center, produced by John Lant and
co-produced by Paul Casey.

*John Lant, Producing Artistic Director

1
HAVE A NICE DAY
A ONE-ACT COMEDY

Cast of Characters

Audrey

     late 20's-early 30's, supervisor

Kenneth

     late 20's-early 30's, musician

Rachel

     late 20's, dramatic

Customer

     late 30's or older, impatient

Scene

A low-cost gift shop.

Time

A few minutes before the shop opens.

AT RISE

KENNETH, obviously lacking sleep, sits behind the counter reading a music magazine. A radio plays. AUDREY, dressed in upscale casual and wearing a name tag and store apron, enters from stock room carrying a small counter display.

AUDREY: Move over, Kenneth.

KENNETH: *(turning off music)* What's this?

AUDREY: Lina ordered it for the counter.

> *(She places unit on cluttered counter next to the register)*

KENNETH: Perfect. You know, I'm thinking of making a little wooden door with a flip up window. Customers will have to give a secret knock to get any service around here.

> *(AUDREY is staring into space.)*

KENNETH: *(knocking on counter)* Hello, Audrey?

AUDREY: Sorry. My students kept me late last night.

KENNETH: Isn't this the senior citizen's class?

> *(RACHEL appears at shop door; AUDREY crosses to door with key.)*

AUDREY: It was the first night with the live nude model.

KENNETH: That was more than I needed to know.

(RACHEL enters from outside, upset.)

RACHEL: Son of a-

AUDREY: Rachel....

RACHEL: -beehive. Stuck behind a bus the entire way over here.

AUDREY: Well, we've got donuts in the back.

RACHEL: Oh, good. And my rent went up. I almost called in today, I'm so upset. Of course, it happens right after my fencing accident.

KENNETH: Sorry to hear it, sister.

RACHEL: Well, he's out of ICU. I need another job.

KENNETH: You need another hobby.

RACHEL: *(pulling a curling iron out of her bag)* I can't believe I've been here a year and haven't had a single raise.

AUDREY: Believe me, it's not worth it.

RACHEL: Where's an outlet? I have to do my hair. *(to*

KENNETH) Oh, sorry I couldn't make it Friday night. I had to help my sister with a cupcake catering emergency. So, how'd it go?

KENNETH: The Finger Puppets were tight. And this junior exec. hung out for two hours dangling his record company in front of us.

RACHEL: Wow, you guys are really getting noticed.

KENNETH: He noticed the drinks we were buying him.

(There is a knock at the door; a man can be seen outside looking in.)

KENNETH: We're not open yet, right?

AUDREY: I've got three minutes till.

(The knocking persists; KENNETH steps over to the door and speaks in exaggerated mime.)

KENNETH: We open at ten.

(CUSTOMER points at wrist.)

KENNETH: Yeah, ten o'clock. Three minutes.

(CUSTOMER shakes head, points at wrist, mouthing the word 'Now'.)

KENNETH: Son of a... Jerk wants the doors open.

AUDREY: Oh, might as well.

(AUDREY gets keys and goes to door.)

RACHEL: What put you in such a good mood?

KENNETH: Long night of band rehearsal.

RACHEL: I was speaking to Audrey.

KENNETH: Oh, excuse me. Her class went late.

RACHEL: I thought she was teaching at the senior
center.

KENNETH: I don't want to talk about it.

RACHEL: All right. If an insurance company calls, I'm
off today.

*(RACHEL exits to stock room;
KENNETH puts his apron on and begins
pricing stock from a box.)*

AUDREY: Good morning.

CUSTOMER: It's after ten.

AUDREY: Sorry.

CUSTOMER: No, you're not. Do you have a

trashcan?

(CUSTOMER hands off a crumpled paper and begins looking around.)

KENNETH: Nice "How do you do".

AUDREY: Is it five yet?

KENNETH: It's happy hour someplace.

AUDREY: I'd settle for a happy five minutes. Right, I'll get those work orders off Lina's desk.

> *(AUDREY exits to stock room, returning with a clipboard of papers; RACHEL enters wearing apron, name tag, and carrying a feather duster.)*

KENNETH: Oh, no, no, no, no. Rachel, will you put that thing away?

RACHEL: What? This? Got a thing for feathers?

KENNETH: That's none of your business. And I want to keep it that way.

RACHEL: Sorry. I have to keep physical to keep my mind off my problems.

> *(CUSTOMER sees her, looks at apron and name tag.)*

CUSTOMER: *(on cell phone)* Hang on a second. *(to RACHEL)* Do you work here?

RACHEL: No. I'm doing community service. See those two people over there, with the aprons? They can help you.

CUSTOMER: Fine. *(to KENNETH)* Do you have books on tape?

KENNETH: We sure don't. Sorry.

CUSTOMER: Right. *(on cell phone)* Yeah, anyway, the reception's lousy in here. I'll have to call you back.

RACHEL: Boy, that felt good.

AUDREY: *(looking through papers)* What the....

KENNETH: What?

AUDREY: *(reading)* "Confirm date with Mystery Shopper."

RACHEL: What kind of moronic name is that? What, are you supposed to guess why they're shopping?

KENNETH: Maybe it's more like Sherlock Holmes in Neiman Marcus.

RACHEL: The Case of the Needless Mark-Up.

AUDREY: No, it's a fake customer, they come in, buy something they don't need with someone else's money and the whole time they're checking out your eye contact and how much you smile at them, and then they fill out a report on your customer service and send it back to the store.

KENNETH: So, a well-kept pervert, whose own job is so idiotic that he has to do it incognito, is judging us on our sex appeal on the job?

AUDREY: Yup.

KENNETH: Got it.

RACHEL: Unbelievable. I mean, this is my job. It's me making money so I can have my life. It's not my life. This job is not my life!

KENNETH: Just keep telling yourself that.

RACHEL: This is ridiculous! Our own manager sends a spy to check up on us? In THIS place? What is wrong with her?

KENNETH: We agreed never to try to answer that.

AUDREY: Will you two be quiet! He could be the guy!

KENNETH: He did make us open on time.

RACHEL: He's rude. He's stupid.

AUDREY: He's a customer, nonetheless. We'll just have to make sure he has no complaints.

RACHEL: How?

KENNETH: Uh, pucker up.

RACHEL: Are you kidding? I have to kiss up to that?

KENNETH: We realize it's a step above your usual clientele, but we're confident you can pull it off.

RACHEL: Audrey, I'm gonna kill him.

AUDREY: Well, do it in the stock room. I don't want this guy to see any employee tension. And look happy. *(to CUSTOMER, smiling)* Can I help you find something?

CUSTOMER: I want to see that hat up there.

AUDREY: Sure. I'll just get the ladder. I'll be right back.

> *(AUDREY exits to the stock room, returning with ladder; CUSTOMER browses at a table with identical items; he picks up items one by one and looks at the prices.)*

RACHEL: *(to CUSTOMER)* Are you finding everything okay?

CUSTOMER: I got a girl helping me.

RACHEL: Okay. *(to KENNETH)* Kenneth. Look what he's doing. Why is he doing that?

KENNETH: I don't know. Maybe he's one of those compulsive people.

RACHEL: A compulsive Mystery Shopper? There's one for the couch.

AUDREY: *(on ladder)* Which hat did you want to see?

CUSTOMER: Oh. I changed my mind.

AUDREY: Oh. No problem. You finished pricing those, Kenneth? Great. Let's get them on the floor.

(AUDREY puts ladder away.)

KENNETH: *(smiling)* Yes ma'am.

CUSTOMER: Hey, don't you guys have complimentary coffee here?

KENNETH: *(smiling)* Absolutely. I'll go get you some. *(to RACHEL)* He wants a cup of coffee.

RACHEL: I think there's still some instant in the back.

KENNETH: I'll go make it.

RACHEL: You don't drink coffee.

KENNETH: So. Is there some reason I can't make it?

RACHEL: Yeah. You don't drink it.

KENNETH: I'll be right back.

RACHEL: Hey, Audrey. What if he's not the Mystery
Shopper?

AUDREY: What if he is?

RACHEL: Yeah, but what if he isn't? And I'm just
being nice to a jerk who's got nothing to do
with my career?

AUDREY: Rachel, we work in a store. Nothing here
has anything to do with your career. Whatever
that turns out to be.

> *(KENNETH enters with paper cup and a
> smile.)*

KENNETH: Here you go, Sir. *(pulling items out of
pocket)* Sugar? Cream? Stirrer?

CUSTOMER: Uh, no thanks.*(takes a sip of coffee
and spits it out.)* Oh, that's disgusting!

KENNETH: *(smiling)* I'm so sorry you're unhappy
with the beverage. Here, let me help you. *(using
his tie as a napkin)* There you go.

CUSTOMER: Get away from me, Punk.

KENNETH: *(smiling)* I understand your anger at me. Allow me to dispose of this for you.

RACHEL: I'm just saying, people who don't drink coffee….

CUSTOMER: (holding up t-shirt) Do you have this in a double extra large?

KENNETH: *(smiling)* I believe we do. Let me -

CUSTOMER: Yeah, check for me.

KENNETH: *(exiting to stock room)* My face hurts.

AUDREY: *(a stack of paper in her hands)* This doesn't look right.

RACHEL: What are they?

AUDREY: Extra job applications. Some of them are filled out.

RACHEL: So?

AUDREY: So, we are fully staffed. And now this Mystery Shopper? I think one of us is getting replaced.

RACHEL: I don't believe her. Oh, poor Kenneth.

AUDREY: Rachel, how do you know it's Kenneth?

RACHEL: You think she's replacing me? Why would she replace me? What did I do?

AUDREY: Well, you know, she could be replacing me.

RACHEL: Yeah. Audrey you're her right arm. You're the right side of her brain, for Pete's sake. She couldn't run this place without you.

AUDREY: Well, eventually she'll have to. I mean, one of these days I'll be moving on. I hope.

KENNETH: *(with t-shirt in hand, smiling)* I knew we had one. Perseverance pays off.

CUSTOMER: *(pulls out wallet)* What's the damage?

RACHEL: *(to AUDREY)* Oh good, that means he's leaving. *(to CUSTOMER)* I can help you here. At the register.

> *(KENNETH and AUDREY fall in line behind counter; RACHEL rings, KENNETH folds, AUDREY bags.)*

RACHEL: Twelve ninety-nine. Please.

> *(CUSTOMER tosses crumpled twenty-dollar bill onto counter.)*

RACHEL: So, it'll be cash. A little wrinkled. No

problem.

(RACHEL pulls curling iron out from below counter and runs the bill through it a few times.)

RACHEL: There we go. All crispy new again. It's a twenty. That makes your change seven oh one. Thank you so much. Here's your receipt.

CUSTOMER: You can throw that away. Hey, I want to look at that hat again.

AUDREY: Sure. I'll just get the ladder.

RACHEL: *(to KENNETH)* Hey, did you know Lina's replacing one of us?

KENNETH: What are you talking about?

RACHEL: *(tidying KENNETH'S appearance)* Audrey just told me. I think Lina sent this guy over to see which one of us gets the boot.

KENNETH: *(fighting off the feather duster)* Will you stop?

RACHEL: Kenneth, I like you. I don't want to see you lose your job. Here, let's fix your hair.

(RACHEL licks her fingers.)

KENNETH: Get away from me!

RACHEL: I want to help you! Stand still a minute!

(AUDREY enters with the ladder; KENNETH struggles to fight off RACHEL, who accidentally pokes him in the eye.)

KENNETH: Ow! Son of a-

RACHEL: Shit! I'm sorry!

AUDREY: *(to CUSTOMER)* Excuse me. *(to RACHEL and KENNETH)* What happened?

KENNETH: She poked my eye out!

AUDREY: Like this place was ever fun and games. Can we please try and look somewhat professional here.

RACHEL: That's what I was trying to do!

KENNETH: Oh! We're smiling our butts off while you strut around like some pre-menstrual peacock!

RACHEL: I rang him up!

KENNETH: *(holding his hand over his eye)* Could someone please get a Band-Aid, or something?

AUDREY: I'll be right back. *(regarding feather duster)* Keep that thing to yourself. *(to CUSTOMER)* Be right with you!

CUSTOMER: Never mind.

> *(CUSTOMER is at table where a sign reads 'All Items On Table Five Dollars'; he picks something up.)*

CUSTOMER: How much is this?

KENNETH: Is it off that table?

CUSTOMER: Yeah.

KENNETH: Well, I guess it's five dollars, then, isn't it. I mean, if it's off the Five Dollar table.

RACHEL: Kenneth! I'm so sorry. He's just had a little accident.

KENNETH: There's a sign, clearly marked. Even I can read it.

CUSTOMER: You need to do something about your attitude, kid. If you want to work in this business, you're going to have to learn some people-pleasing skills.

KENNETH: I hate having to say this to you, but you're right.

RACHEL: *("dusting" herself to distract KENNETH)* Kenneth...

AUDREY: *(grabbing feather duster)* Give me that.

KENNETH: You're an ass, but you're right. My attitude needed that adjustment. There's only one person I'm concerned about pleasing. And you're not it. *(to AUDREY)* Thanks.

(KENNETH takes cloth from AUDREY and exits at door.)

CUSTOMER: I don't believe this place.

AUDREY: I apologize. That was very unprofessional and I'll be speaking to him about...

CUSTOMER: Don't apologize to me anymore. Nobody's sorry about anything. I just want to finish up my business here. Give me the hat.

AUDREY: I'll be happy to get it for you.

RACHEL: I'll help you. *(whispering)* This is crazy! Why won't he leave? Doesn't he have enough on us?

AUDREY: We're almost there. Don't fall apart on me. Lina lost a lot of points with this one. *(handing hat to CUSTOMER)* Here you are.

CUSTOMER: Oh, this sucks. Forget it.

AUDREY: Okay. No problem.

(AUDREY climbs up and down the ladder replacing the hat.)

RACHEL: It was a pleasure doing business with you. Come ba- Have a nice day.

CUSTOMER: No, changed my mind, again. Give it to me.

(AUDREY climbs ladder again.)

CUSTOMER: Truth is, I just enjoy watching a girl climbing her way to the top.

AUDREY: Oh, hey, that's funny. I'm putting the ladder away, now. Do you want the hat?

CUSTOMER: Are you being smart with me?

AUDREY: I don't see how that's possible.

CUSTOMER: I'd like to see your manager.

AUDREY: She's not in today.

CUSTOMER: Well, she's getting a call.

AUDREY: Why? Because somehow you're qualified to determine whether or not I'm good enough to work here? Don't threaten me. I'm tired. Tired of playing by the rules and being miserable, tired of climbing ladders and never getting to the top. And I'm sick and tired of wasting my time with you.

(AUDREY exits to stock room.)

RACHEL: I - what a crazy day, huh? That's a very nice shirt you're wearing. Well, except for the coffee part.

(AUDREY enters with her purse and crosses to door.)

AUDREY: Sorry, Rach, you'll have to wrap this one up on your own.

RACHEL: Wait. Audrey. You can't mean that. Don't leave me here. I-Audrey-wait! *(to CUSTOMER)* I'd like to offer you a very generous discount on that hat.

CUSTOMER: Finally, some customer service. Of course, I won't mention this unauthorized discount to your manager. Could you hurry it up, though? I have to get to the law office.

RACHEL: Oh. You're a lawyer.

CUSTOMER: No. My brother was involved in an accident.

RACHEL: Oh, I'm so sorr-. What happened?

CUSTOMER: Some idiot nearly skewered his eye in his fencing class. I can't wait to go to court.

RACHEL: Holy milk and crackers!

CUSTOMER: What's the matter?

RACHEL: I think Audrey left the stock room light on. Excuse me.

> *(RACHEL exits to stock room;*
> *CUSTOMER takes out cell phone;*
> *RACHEL enters with purse, running for the*
> *door.)*

CUSTOMER: Hey, what about my discount?

RACHEL: A hundred percent off today!

CUSTOMER: *(on cell phone)* Hello, Lina Munson? Tony Curran. All finished here...Yeah, all three...Oh, I think Rachel will land on her feet, if she doesn't land on someone else's first...Don't start doubting yourself. They'll be all right. They've got better things to do with their lives, and now they know it. I'll lock up and wait for you outside...You're very welcome...Are you kidding? I wouldn't trade this job for the world! See you soon.

> *(CUSTOMER exits.)*

CURTAIN

J. M. KESSLER

2
THE TIN HEART
A ONE-ACT ROMANCE

Cast of Characters

Minette Keath

>30's, a pleasant, positive-minded woman, works part-time for the local Weekly Beacon

Josiah Keath

>40's-50's, building inspector, embittered writer

Percival Adamson

>youthful indeterminate age, peculiar owner of a recycling business

Scene

Interior of Josiah and Minette's home.

SETTING

The main room is cozy and comfortable with a corner office, front door SL, a closet, and a small kitchen/bar. The bedroom and bathroom are indicated off SR. There are drapes and a book shelf with books.

AT RISE

MINETTE is putting assorted items and boxes back into the closet. One box is on the coffee table, as is an old brief case with a key lock. JOSIAH enters unseen, burdened with brief case, mail, flowers, etc.

MINETTE: I don't get it. There's one less box. Why doesn't this work?

JOSIAH: Nature of the universe, as I understand it.

MINETTE: Joe! You scared me.

JOSIAH: Sorry, Min. *(presents flowers)*

MINETTE: They're beautiful, Honey. Thank you.

> *(MINETTE kisses Josiah, takes the flowers and puts them in a vase.)*

JOSIAH: Yeah, happy anniversary.
(Looking through mail) I'm still getting letters from that book club. I haven't ordered anything in, I don't even know how many years. You'd think they'd get a clue. What's all this - what are you doing?

MINETTE: I was looking for something. I wanted to reorganize it, anyway. How was work today?

JOSIAH: You're always moving things around. Why

do you do that?

MINETTE: Because I'm good at it.

JOSIAH: I can't find anything when you clean. Like
my socks. I couldn't find my socks this
morning. I open the drawer - no socks. I don't
like wondering where my socks are at six in the
morning.

MINETTE: Oh, I relined all the drawers.

JOSIAH: At six o'clock this morning?

MINETTE: No, yesterday. I must have put things
back wrong, sorry. Oh, I need your help in the
- no, I put them in the top drawer, I
remember.

JOSIAH: Yeah, but I like them in the bottom drawer,
they're closer to my feet. (*Reading mail*) What is
this trend with adult writers now, everyone
writing for kids?

MINETTE: (*Struggling at the closet*)
Why don't you order something and find out.

JOSIAH: Min, you want some help with that?

MINETTE: I got it. It's just this, here.

JOSIAH: What's that box?

MINETTE: Oh, that's something.... So, what
    happened at work?

*(During the following, JOSIAH notices his
old briefcase, finds it locked. He can't
remember what he has done with the key.
JOSIAH crosses to office and puts his old
briefcase on his desk.)*

JOSIAH: Oh, the usual. After retraining a band of
    elephant poachers for positions in the U. N., I
    rid the world of spammers, and then returned
    to my office, where I finally succumbed to the
    charms of my assistant, Plenty Goodallover.
    (Pause) I had to inspect a new building with
    the new owners. At the end of it all they were
    missing a permit, so, I get to meet with them
    again on Monday.

MINETTE: There was a briefcase here, what did I do
    with it?

JOSIAH: Oh, I, uh, that was my old one, forgot I still
    had it.

MINETTE: Oh. I took care of the car today. And I
    picked up a new showerhead, but I couldn't get
    the old one off.

JOSIAH: I'll take a look at it later. We've got
    reservations for tonight.

MINETTE: I know, so let me go, uh, you know.

Fifteen minutes. And I need your help....

JOSIAH: Yeah, be right there.

(MINETTE exits SR.)

(JOSIAH takes out his old briefcase, thinks better of it, and puts it back. He crosses to coffee table to put the box away. It's heavy; he opens it and reveals an old black typewriter, decorated to suggest medieval romance.)

(MINETTE enters SR.)

MINETTE: You know, there's that new bar downtown, maybe after dinner we could...

JOSIAH: I thought I got rid of it.

MINETTE: You did. I didn't. I couldn't.

JOSIAH: Why did you do this, Minette? I didn't want it anymore. I told you.

MINETTE: I know what you said, and why you did it, and I figured you'd come to regret it later. You don't throw something like that away. Besides, Sir Remington here delivered your proposal to me. I thought it would be romantic tonight.

JOSIAH: It isn't.

MINETTE: Well, give it a minute. It always needed

time to warm up.

JOSIAH: It's a worn out steel-plated burden! A museum piece. You should have left it where you found it. You should have respected my decision and left it at that!
(pause) Thanks for getting the oil changed. I'll take a look at the shower tomorrow, I don't want to get messed up before dinner. How was the staff today?

MINETTE: I just had some editing so I e-mailed the Weekly Beacon from here. And I was on the phone with your mom for quite a while.

JOSIAH: Oh. Did you have a nice listen?

MINETTE: I like hearing her stories about you. She likes to remember, it's sweet. And she likes me to reassure her that I'm taking care of you. And that you're taking care of me. What time is the reservation?

JOSIAH: Six. There's a game on at eight, so.... Or, was there was something you wanted to watch?

MINETTE: No, there's nothing. I guess I'll go get cleaned up.

JOSIAH: Minette, I'm sorry, but, you throw it at me after all these years, how did you think I'd react?

MINETTE: I don't know. I guess I thought that life-long dreams were just that; something you built your life around. Our life.

JOSIAH: If it means so much to you, keep it. Use it for a potted plant or something.

MINETTE: I don't need a potted plant, Joe.

JOSIAH: I'm sure you'll find some use for it.

MINETTE: Well at least you're consulting me this time. You know what, fine. It's gone.

(Doorbell.)

JOSIAH: It was gone six years ago.

(JOSIAH answers the door - a man with a clipboard and blue recycling bin is revealed.)

PERCIVAL: Hello. Here for the recycling.

JOSIAH: Excuse me?

(PERCIVAL produces a business card from out of nowhere, much like a parlor trick.)

PERCIVAL: Percival Adamson, Redeemables.

JOSIAH: Redeemables?

PERCIVAL: I thought it had a more hopeful sound to

it. You've got a typewriter, black, not seen the
light of day in six years, listed here as
57M94/Q. Sir Remington Something? I'm here
to collect. 211 Longfellow Drive? Friday?

JOSIAH: Yeah. (To MINETTE) You did this?

MINETTE: I didn't call him.

PERCIVAL: Well, this really puts me in a spot. Unless
I've got the time screwed up. Am I here at the
wrong time?

JOSIAH: Oh, no. My wife was just dragging me
through the mud of memory lane.

MINETTE: It's right over here. Do you need a hand
with it? Joe, give him a hand with it.

JOSIAH: I don't believe this.

MINETTE: I said I didn't call him.

JOSIAH: Oh, some guy just happens to show up on
our anniversary and happens to know all about
Sir Remington here, but you have no idea who
he is.

MINETTE: Evidently he's a godsend, solving all our
problems.

(PERCIVAL crosses to typewriter.)

31

PERCIVAL: Wow, look at that. It's a classic. Looks in good shape, too. mind if I, uh...

(PERCIVAL strikes one key.)

PERCIVAL: I love that sound.

JOSIAH: Look, who sent you here?

MINETTE: What difference does it make? You want it gone, he wants to take it. I'll get the door.

JOSIAH: And this meant so much to you a minute ago.

MINETTE: Yeah, well, there's been a change of heart.

PERCIVAL: Sounds like you're having second thoughts, Joe.

JOSIAH: I'm not having second thoughts. She's the one who kept this...

PERCIVAL: Great. If you two could just sign here. Someone will be really happy to get this.

JOSIAH: You're going to give this to just anyone?

PERCIVAL: I don't see where that concerns you.

JOSIAH: Excuse me. That's a collector's piece.

MINETTE: I thought it was a worn out steel-plated

burden. I think I'll skip dinner, Joe.

(MINETTE exits SR.)

PERCIVAL: "...the sons of God saw the daughters of men that they were fair...." Will she be gone long? I'll need her signature as well.

JOSIAH: *(At bar)* Would you like one? Have one. We're celebrating.

PERCIVAL: What's the occasion?

JOSIAH: Here, let me sign that. We'll drink, and you can be on your way.

(PERCIVAL produces a large quill pen from out of nowhere.)

JOSIAH: Is the prestidigitation for your own amusement?

PERCIVAL: Sorry. Bit of a habit.

JOSIAH: So, Percival? Percy?

PERCIVAL: Pierce.

JOSIAH: Pierce. What is it with women saving everything? They get attached to "things," they can't let go. You should see the closets around here; you need a hard hat just to hang up your coat. I don't have a problem letting go of things, do you? I mean, I can't believe she's had it in this house all this time! When I told her. She knew.

PERCIVAL: Who's idea was knighthood?

JOSIAH: Minette's. We used to have this...idea...I don't know, it was stupid. I don't know why I'm telling you all this. I'm sorry, I don't mean to unload on you.

PERCIVAL: Go on.

JOSIAH: It's "Sir Remington, Able to Pierce Publishing Houses in One Page." She said something about guaranteeing it serve faithfully, or die trying.

PERCIVAL: Women. Helpless romantics.

JOSIAH: I think it's, "hopeless."

PERCIVAL: Oh, I don't know about that.

(PERCIVAL places a hand on JOSIAH'S shoulder, and a brief and subtle lighting change happens. JOSIAH notices something briefly, but dismisses it.)

PERCIVAL: So, you're a writer.

JOSIAH: Just lived like one for a while. I mistook talent for vocation.

PERCIVAL: What did you write?

JOSIAH: A sort of science fiction noir.

PERCIVAL: Did you always want to be a writer?

JOSIAH: I was always good at it. I enjoyed it. Yeah.
Published in magazines regularly, short stories.
I had this studio apartment after college...it was
an interesting life. For a while.

PERCIVAL: But you were longing for a suit and tie,
with a briefcase full of security. I think you
mistook boredom for responsibility. What
about Min?

JOSIAH: What about her?

PERCIVAL: I don't know. Did she always want to be
married to you?

JOSIAH: What? I don't, I....

PERCIVAL: I just wondered if she had any other
interests in life. Not that marriage isn't
interesting.

JOSIAH: Min studied anthropology. She wanted to
travel, live in different places, study people.

PERCIVAL: Did she?

JOSIAH: We had just returned from a trip to Mexico,

and I asked her to marry me. So she took a job at the Natural History Museum for a while, until we got settled in.

PERCIVAL: And her dream of a peripatetic life?

JOSIAH: We've been places, we've taken trips. And she's got her paper, she's happy. I never told her what to do, she decided for herself. That's who she is.

PERCIVAL: It's nice that way. I mean, when you know someone, it's something you can count on.

JOSIAH: Right.

PERCIVAL: The way you can count on going to work every day. I like writers. The written word. There's something about putting something down on paper; the things you think about, the thoughts you toy with, the secret, haunted parts of yourself decoded in black and white, and then someone reads all that, someone brings you into their mind, to consort with all of their thoughts, and you're connected, through ink and paper. Such mundane things become so powerfully intimate. *(Pause)* Sorry, I find it fascinating.

JOSIAH: Yeah, well people have to read your work for that to happen. Even then, it doesn't always happen. So, what do you say we close the book on that.

PERCIVAL: As you wish. *(while Josiah signs)* Josiah Keath. Dangerous name for a writer.

JOSIAH: Why is that?

PERCIVAL: Josiah means "Fire of the Lord." And Keath is Welsh for forest.

JOSIAH: I see what you mean. Well, all my self-destructive behavior makes sense to me now. Thank you. Nothing like a little truth to see the light.

PERCIVAL: "He who knows others is wise; he who knows himself is enlightened."

JOSIAH: Hallelujah.

PERCIVAL: The key to bliss.

> *(They touch glasses and drink. PERCIVAL coughs up a key.)*

PERCIVAL: Oh, no.

JOSIAH: You coughed up a key.

PERCIVAL: Yeah. I wonder what it's for. It looks like one of those old -

JOSIAH: Hey, wait a second, let me see that. Oh, no, it couldn't be.

(JOSIAH goes to his old brief case. The key unlocks it.)

JOSIAH: How did you get this key? Who are you? What is it you want here?

PERCIVAL: It was an accident, I didn't mean to do that when I said that, but then you said, too. If you could both just sign here, I can leave you in peace.

JOSIAH: Look, I want the truth! Did you just say, "leave you in peace?"

PERCIVAL: That's generally what we do.

JOSIAH: Uh-huh. *(figures something out)* Mom. You're one of those, this whole thing, she called you - you're not going to strip, are you?

PERCIVAL: No. I'm just here for the recycling. It's my final rescue, a hundred and fifty-seven points, I just need your wife's signature.

JOSIAH: All right. So, sorry, you've got your own business but you need points?

PERCIVAL: I have a quota to meet. Time's up tonight. Wow, the whole "time" thing, it's weird to me the way you break it down into these segments that get smaller and smaller and smaller only they never disappear because you keep adding them up so you can have more of these little segments of time and you try to fit as many of the little segments into the bigger segments as you can because you don't want to waste any of them and then you have this pressure to fill each segment of time with as much as you can because somehow that saves it. Only I haven't figured out yet where it all gets stored. Well, I'm glad I don't have to live with it. I mean I won't after this. (Pause) You're having trouble with this, aren't you, Josiah? Is it because I'm not cherubic?

(The drapes close.)

PERCIVAL: Or luminous?

(A light flickers.)

PERCIVAL: Although, technically...

(A book falls off a shelf.)

PERCIVAL: ...haloes are the result of a fourth century artist movement. Many people don't know that.

JOSIAH: I'm, I, I, I, I mean, you, you, you...with the, the...and then the, thing with the...you, no, no,

it's something, it's like...you're a, you're a
psycho-kinetic magician.

PERCIVAL: Just living like one, for a while. Josiah,
must I spell it out for you?

JOSIAH: You expect me to believe that...you're....
Right.

PERCIVAL: Why is it they always wish it would
happen to them, and then when it does, they
just won't believe it?

JOSIAH: So you're saying, you're an..., from On High,
and all that?

PERCIVAL: Do you need more proof?

*(A warm light surrounds the both of them; it
seems to be alive. Josiah is overwhelmed by the
power flowing through him. The effect ends.)*

JOSIAH: Am I in big trouble?

PERCIVAL: Oh, no, no, no, no, no, no. You're
thinking of Azreal. Archangel. I'm just the
common variety. Although we are in the same
triad. Third. I'm just here for the signatures
and a hundred and fifty-seven points.

JOSIAH: Do you mind if I have another...?

PERCIVAL: No. Do you mind if I don't join you?

JOSIAH: No. No. No. So, what, you get your points and then you fly up to the Pearly Gates?

PERCIVAL: No. We use the servants entrance.

JOSIAH: Of, course. What's this quota you have?

PERCIVAL: Five hundred million and three.

JOSIAH: Jesus!

(PERCIVAL turns around in near panic.)

JOSIAH: I'm sorry. So, where are you at?

PERCIVAL: Four hundred ninety-nine million, nine-hundred ninety-nine thousand, eight hundred and forty-six.

JOSIAH: Well, what, I mean, if it's not too personal, I didn't know you could do anything wrong.

PERCIVAL: Wrong? I don't know that it was wrong. It was a choice, followed by a consequence. I was sent to answer a prayer, and when I saw her, I wanted very much to be the answer. I incarnated. We all do it, temporarily, from time to time, disguise ourselves as humans. "Be not forgetful to entertain strangers; for thereby..."

JOSIAH: "...some have entertained angels unawares."

PERCIVAL: She cast aside her dreams because of me. It caused a disturbance in the scheme of things.

JOSIAH: So, there is a divine plan?

PERCIVAL: Well, yes. But you'd be surprised at how many things are set on random. Of course, they were destined to be set on random.

JOSIAH: I thought all you had to do was say you're sorry?

PERCIVAL: No. You must forgive the cause of your sorrow.

JOSIAH: Doesn't seem like much of a punishment.

PERCIVAL: It's almost a fascination with your kind, regarding a life-lesson as punishment.

JOSIAH: Well, they often feel like that. So, if this, what you're doing, if it's not a punishment, then why do you need to have that collected by tonight?

PERCIVAL: Window of opportunity. It closes tonight. I elected to stay here, to take on this work. After tonight, it's no longer a choice.

JOSIAH: You certainly make it sound like you don't like being here.

PERCIVAL: Never to be home again? Everyday reminded of that, and everyday unable to forget why it isn't so.

JOSIAH: I guess, in your case there really is no place like home.

PERCIVAL: Home isn't a place to us, it's a state of being. For you, it's human being. And I must say, that's a lot to be.

JOSIAH: I can't blame you for wanting your wings back.

PERCIVAL: It's the gravity down here, the weight of responsibility. Really overwhelming at times. But then, you're born to it.

JOSIAH: I'm not so sure that it makes it any easier. What's it like? When you're, home? Is it, like that? *(referencing the light)*

PERCIVAL: Do you remember the moment that you knew you were in love? *(Pause)* It's that moment, times infinity.

JOSIAH: So, is all of this because I never believed?

PERCIVAL: We don't mind if you don't believe in us. We're not offended by it. It's when you don't believe in yourself that you're in trouble. That's the real offence, because you hurt more than just yourself.

JOSIAH: And that's why you're here, to protect the greater good-

PERCIVAL: We're just here, watching things.
(MINETTE enters SR.)

MINETTE: Would you mind looking at the shower.

JOSIAH: Min, I-

MINETTE: Please.

JOSIAH: Yeah. Sure. Look, he, um, he needs to - the thing is, he...Well, he'll explain everything. *(To Percival)* You'll explain everything, won't you?

PERCIVAL: Min needs your help, Joe.

(JOSIAH exits SR taking his old brief case with him.)

MINETTE: I'm sorry, I thought you'd left already. Aren't you taking this?

PERCIVAL: Sure. If you could just sign here.

MINETTE: Didn't Josiah sign it?

PERCIVAL: I need signatures from both parties.

MINETTE: I don't know why you want to give this away. You could get a lot of money for it. I mean without the decorations.

PERCIVAL: It's not about the money. I collect broken dreams and recycle them. Can I let you in on a secret?

MINETTE: Of, course.

PERCIVAL: Dreams always come true, even if you abandon them. When that happens, they just come true for someone else. That's why I'm here.

MINETTE: I see. So, Percy?

PERCIVAL: Percival.

MINETTE: I like it. It suits you. So, you believe in "happily ever afters", Percival?

PERCIVAL: It's kind of an occupational hazard.

MINETTE: We had it coming to us. The storybook romance with the fairytale ending. We struggled, but we knew where we were headed. We could always just see it on the horizon, that sunset we were riding into. Then one critic slammed him.

(JOSIAH enters SR unseen with old brief case.)

MINETTE: Said his material read like a "lovesick antiquity". One critic. You know I pulled that out of the trash. I kept it at his mother's house for a couple of years, I didn't dare risk him finding it here. Why are men so stubborn? And selfish. He tears his heart out, locks it up and throws it away! Only he forgot that it's not his to dispose of. He forgot about the day that he gave his heart to me.

(MINETTE signs the form.)

JOSIAH: I was trying to protect you. I wanted you to be the wife of a successful, well-respected man, not some joke of a writer in the Book Review. I was embarrassed. I couldn't write, and you took a job to pay the bills. Not the life we dreamed of.

(JOSIAH opens the old brief case. He takes out a manuscript and gives it to MINETTE.)

JOSIAH: I started writing it when the first book was being published. I put it away when the review came out.

MINETTE: *(reading)* "For Minette, my Faithful Defender".

JOSIAH: I've kept this locked up long enough. Forgive me?

MINETTE: I did, a long time ago. You've just never forgiven yourself.

(PERCIVAL crosses to door with typewriter.)

JOSIAH: Hey, wait a minute with that.

(JOSIAH crosses to typewriter, pauses, and strikes one key.)

JOSIAH: Go home, Pierce. And thank you.

PERCIVAL: My pleasure.

(As PERCIVAL steps into the threshold with the typewriter, a warm, white light shines on him. PERCIVAL disappears.)

MINETTE: Josiah, did you see that? It's just that, it looked like he walked into...

(JOSIAH kisses MINETTE.)

JOSIAH: I think we may have lost our dinner reservation. Fortunately, my assistant made contingency plans at a very exclusive, local refrigerator.

MINETTE: She sounds efficient, this Miss Goodallover. Does she cook, too?

JOSIAH: Her only flaw. But I hear the Chef's Special is all the rage. Care to sample it?

MINETTE: I need your help flipping the mattress.

JOSIAH: Minette. You're always moving things.

MINETTE: I'm good that way.

JOSIAH: You're pure joy. Times Infinity.

CURTAIN

3
A ROSE BY ANY OTHER NAME
A RADIO PLAY

Cast of Characters

Michael

>mid- to late-thirties, civil engineer,
brother of

David

>mid- to late-thirties, educational toy
development director

Scene

Two brothers are driving to their mother's house on
Mother's Day.

AT RISE

The actors stand in front of microphones with their scripts.

> *(SFX: CAR DRIVING AMBIANCE*
> *PLAYS THROUGHOUT)*

MICHAEL: Red roses. They are beautiful.

DAVID: I still say they should be yellow.

MICHAEL: David, for the last time, yellow
    symbolizes friendship, red symbolizes deep
    love.

DAVID: Right. But I think it's for a more intimate
    kind of love, not the kind of love someone has
    for their mother.

MICHAEL: It's not restrictive. Love is love no matter
    who you have it for.

DAVID: I just think that Mom would prefer
    something brighter, you know, like springtime
    colors. Besides, isn't pink supposed to be the
    "new red"?

MICHAEL: What the hell are you talking about?

DAVID: I don't know. I overheard it at Starbucks.
    You sure the flowers aren't getting crushed?

MICHAEL: Yeah, they're fine.

DAVID: Okay. Are the gifts okay? I don't want them sliding around the back seat.

MICHAEL: They're fine. I fastened them in with the seat belts.

DAVID: You what? Michael, for God's sake! That'll crush the paper!

MICHAEL: Crush the paper? Where'd my brother go? Because I thought he was sitting here beside me just a second ago.

DAVID: I just don't want to give mom a wrinkly present.

MICHAEL: Did you just use the word wrinkly?

DAVID: It's just ...I ...I'm....

MICHAEL: What?

DAVID: I want everything to be right.

MICHAEL: You mean perfect.

DAVID: Look. It's a very special day. Not just for Mom, for us too. I mean this year especially.

MICHAEL: Exactly, that's why I came up with the idea to *bring* dinner. You brought the gifts, I brought the food and flowers, we're covered. So, just relax.

DAVID: You're right.

MICHAEL: It's going to be a great day.

DAVID: It is.

> *(DAVID SIGHS ... AFTER A BEAT HE STARTS TO CHUCKLE)*

MICHAEL: What?

DAVID: Wrinkly.

> *(BOTH SHARE A LAUGH)*

DAVID: We've never had lobster on Mother's Day before, right?

MICHAEL: Nope. Just wait until she opens that ice cooler and sees those babies just waitin' for a hot bath and a lemon butter rubdown. You remember that vacation when we all went out on that fishing boat?

DAVID: Yeah, worst vacation of my life, and thanks for bringing it up.

MICHAEL: As I recall you were the one bringing it up, if you know what I mean.

DAVID: Hey, I was seven.

MICHAEL: That was the first time I had lobster.

DAVID: Wasn't that the same vacation when Mom had that accident? On the bicycle?

MICHAEL: Oh yeah, we rented bikes and some guy went through a stop sign.

DAVID: Mom turned to check on us. Figured that guy was gonna stop, you know, like he was supposed to.

MICHAEL: You know what I remember most is the sound of the impact.

DAVID: Oh man, it was horrible. And seeing Mom on the road, her head was bleeding, the bicycle all bent up. And her leg underneath. I was so mad at that guy I wanted to kill him.

MICHAEL: Tell me about it. Six weeks in the hospital. And Mom said, "Look! You've got a mummy for a mommy!" She never felt sorry for herself. Always found a reason to laugh.

DAVID: We were lucky, to grow up with laughter in the house.

MICHAEL: I don't think I've ever fully appreciated that until now. I'll tell you, the broken leg didn't bother me so much, but seeing her head all bandaged up, I didn't like that.

DAVID: That was evident when you burst into tears.

MICHAEL: Hey ... I was seven.

DAVID: Take it easy. You shouldn't be so uptight about letting out a few emotions.

MICHAEL: Funny, that's just what Jennifer says. I suppose Sandra thinks you're God's gift because you "express yourself".

DAVID: I don't know. But I'm pretty good at communicating with her, yeah.

MICHAEL: Mm.

> *(SFX: A FEW BEATS OF JUST THE CAR MOVING.)*

DAVID: *(CHANGES SUBJECT)* Thirty years. Did you ever imagine you'd be where you are today?

MICHAEL: Well, considering that in the third grade I was sure I was going to work for NASA.

DAVID: Oh yeah, I remember that. Mom was so mad at you for using up all her aluminum foil.

MICHAEL: Yeah, but I was the only one on our block with a fully equipped rocket.

DAVID: That's right, what she got really mad about was the fact that you'd taken about half the kitchen appliances to furnish the inside of the ship, and linked her hair curlers together to make a lifeline so you could float in space.

MICHAEL: No one understood my genius. Anyway, what about you?

DAVID: Oh, I didn't understand it either.

MICHAEL: I meant, did you always know you'd be doing what you're doing?

DAVID: I guess so. I always liked planning things, building things, working things out. Yeah. Although, in high school I thought about going into medicine.

MICHAEL: Really?

DAVID: Yeah, I thought about it for a while. I thought it would be nice for Mom to have a doctor in the family, you know.

MICHAEL: So what changed your mind?

DAVID: I just found that it wasn't my thing.

MICHAEL: Mmm. Wait a minute. Wait, wait, it's all coming back to me now. I had chemistry the same period you had biology. And I remember one day hearing something in the hall, and when I looked up I saw you running. You told me later that Mr. Reinhart sent you on an errand. But at the end of the period, I heard everyone talking - it was you, wasn't it? You couldn't dissect a frog!

DAVID: It was a hot day, I had skipped lunch.

MICHAEL: You puked!

DAVID: Oh give me a break, I was twelve.

MICHAEL: Man, you've got a sensitive stomach. Well it's natural, I mean, seeing the frog there, its guts hanging out. Not for everyone, I guess.

DAVID: Yeah.

MICHAEL: Stomach sliced open, the skin flapped back like opening a door.

DAVID: *(FIGHTS NAUSEA)* Okay, that's enough.

MICHAEL: Oh, sorry.

DAVID: Anyway. I think Mom's happy with what we've made of our lives. A civil engineer, and an educational toy maker.

MICHAEL: Director of Development, thank you.

DAVID: You know, I've always wondered, do you wear red suits and pointy hats when you're making the toys?

MICHAEL: Only for board meetings.

DAVID: Sounds oddly appropriate. Of course, the one other thing that would make Mom happy is...

BOTH: ...If we were married.

MICHAEL: I know. So, things really are good with you and Sandra?

DAVID: Yeah, good. You and Jennifer?

MICHAEL: Yeah, we're good.

DAVID: Good.

MICHAEL: Yeah.

(SFX: ANOTHER FEW BEATS OF JUST THE CAR MOVING)

DAVID: We're getting great gas mileage. Traffic's not too bad either. We'll probably get there a little early.

MICHAEL: These flowers are going to want a long drink of water. We should have bought a vase.

DAVID: I should have thought of that. Well, Mom's got to have some vases.

MICHAEL: Sure.

DAVID: Yeah. *(BEAT)* Did you ever wonder what

kind of lives we might have had, if things had been different?

MICHAEL: You mean without Mom?

DAVID: Right.

MICHAEL: Yeah, I've thought about it. Makes me really grateful for these last thirty years.

DAVID: Me too. Remember that Parents Picnic in middle school?

MICHAEL: I think so, I'm not sure.

DAVID: Mom and I had just finished the obstacle course and Frank Carpenter and his dad were going through it.

MICHAEL: Oh, right! Frankie Carpenter. Mom said he was teaching music theory at State College.

DAVID: Yeah. Anyway, Frank missed a tire and fell over into his dad and they got disqualified. His mother was so mad at him. *(IMITATING FRANK'S MOTHER)* "As if your grades aren't bad enough, Frankie, now you can't even do the obstacle course! I'm so humiliated!"

MICHAEL: I remember he left early. I thought he hurt himself, he looked like he wanted to cry.

DAVID: And then his mother says... *(ALSO*

IMITATING FRANK'S MOM) "I don't know what his problem is. His brother's on the basketball team, his sister is class president; I'm wondering if he's actually our boy at all."

MICHAEL: Oh man, that's harsh.

DAVID: But then mom said, "Maybe he shouldn't be."

MICHAEL: Go, mom.

DAVID: Anyway, I found out years later that after that day, Mom gave Frankie free piano lessons for years.

MICHAEL: And he's teaching music theory now, thanks to her, huh? The sad thing is, it was a chance to get away from his own mom, and spend time with ours. It's such a roll of the dice, it really is, you know. The kind of parents you have. The kind of person you end up becoming because of them.

DAVID: I'm wondering what else she did behind our backs.

MICHAEL: I was just thinking that, too. It's like, she had this secret life. Super Mom, Defender of the Downtrodden. Faster than a high-speed mixer, more powerful than Wednesday night chili con carne, look, up in the sky it's: Our Mom!

DAVID: Spoken like a true toy maker You always were the more happy-go-lucky one. You know if I didn't already have documentation proving you're my brother...

MICHAEL: Hey, speaking of which, the certificates look great. I like how you did the old and new photos around them. Do you think we should have put "Happy Anniversary" on them, too?

DAVID: I thought that would be too much. I like to keep it simple. Besides, the pictures say a lot.

MICHAEL: Especially yours, with that little suitcase next to you, like you wanted to keep it handy, just in case.

DAVID: Hard to believe it now, but I really wasn't convinced that we'd found a permanent home.

MICHAEL: Really? David, I never knew that.

DAVID: I figured we'd last a couple of weeks maybe, then they'd decide that two boys were too much, and we'd have to pack up again. But it wasn't like that at all.

MICHAEL: No, not at all. I had a good feeling that first day, walking up the front steps of the house. It just felt like home to me. And remember Mom crying when she saw us? She was going to pick us up later in the week, but

Mrs. Williams pushed the adoption paperwork
through and brought us over for Mother's Day.

DAVID: I remember her laughing about how the
doctors told her she'd never have children, and
now she had two sons. *(LAUGHS)* And then
she had us help her make dinner, she really
wanted us to feel that we were a family, right
from the start.

MICHAEL: That was one brave woman. Me mashing
potatoes for the first time in my life, and you
trying to flatten out the lumps in the gravy with
a spatula. She didn't even make us wash up
before dinner! How cool was that?

DAVID: She said we were naturally merciless in the
kitchen and that one of us was bound to be
chef. I hope, I hope we've made her proud.

MICHAEL: Yeah, I know. I hope so too. Something
tells me we have.

DAVID: Yeah.

MICHAEL: *(AFTER A PAUSE)* You know, David,
I'm thinking, Jennifer's the one.

DAVID: Really? You guys been talking about it?

MICHAEL: Well, there have been, you know,
indications of something long lasting, yeah.

DAVID: That's great! She's a great girl.

MICHAEL: She is that. So's Sandra.

DAVID: Yes, yes she is. She is.

MICHAEL: So...?

DAVID: So...I've got a ring I've been carrying around for two weeks...

MICHAEL: What? Excuse me, what's the direct quote, now? "Yeah, man, I'm pretty good at communicating with my girlfriend"!

DAVID: Yeah, yeah...

MICHAEL: Two weeks?! Why the hell haven't you asked her?

DAVID: I don't know, I guess I just want that moment to be-

BOTH: Perfect.

DAVID: And I figure this way I can show the ring to Mom today, get her blessing, you know.

MICHAEL: Are you kidding? We've had her blessing from the moment she signed those adoption papers.

DAVID: Yeah, you're right. Our lives have been

blessed.

(SFX CAR TURNS ONTO A GRAVEL ROAD, STARTS TO SLOW)

MICHAEL: Here's the turn. I love this street, so many memories. Okay, I've got the the cooler, you get the flowers and gifts. Ready?

(SFX: CAR COMES TO A STOP, IGNITION OUT)

DAVID: Hang on. Look. Up on the porch.

(MUSIC: IN AND UNDER)

MICHAEL: *(OVERCOME WITH EMOTION)* Our Mom.

DAVID: You were right about the roses. Red is definitely her color.

(MUSIC: THEME UP AND OUT)

CURTAIN

ABOUT THE AUTHOR

J. M. Kessler has a B. A. in Theatre Arts, and has worked in the theatre as a playwright, actor, and technician. She is also the author of the children's book, *The Squirrelly Nut Gig*. Visit at jmkesssler.co.uk.

www.ingramcontent.com/pod-product-compliance
Lightning Source LLC
Chambersburg PA
CBHW060703030426
42337CB00017B/2732